Spot the Differences

Goose or Duck?

by Natalie Deniston

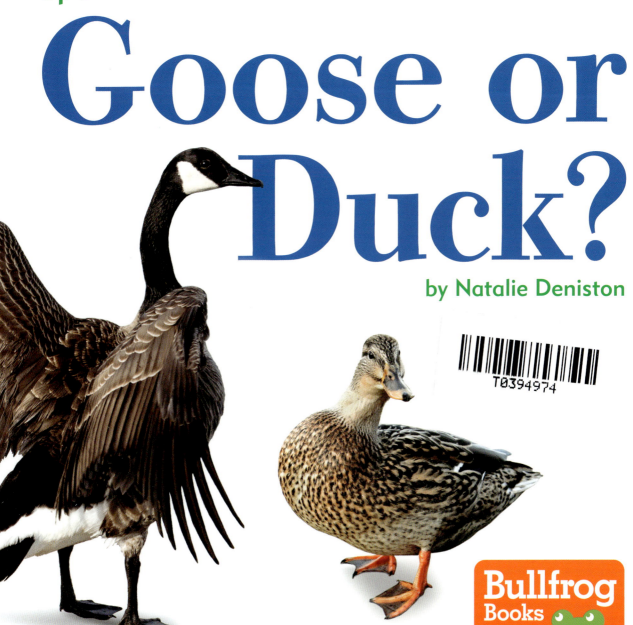

Bullfrog Books

Ideas for Parents and Teachers

Bullfrog Books let children practice reading informational text at the earliest reading levels. Repetition, familiar words, and photo labels support early readers.

Before Reading
- Discuss the cover photo. What does it tell them?
- Look at the picture glossary together. Read and discuss the words.

Read the Book
- "Walk" through the book and look at the photos. Let the child ask questions. Point out the photo labels.
- Read the book to the child, or have them read independently.

After Reading
- Prompt the child to think more. Ask: Have you ever seen a goose or duck? Would you like to?

Bullfrog Books are published by Jump!
5357 Penn Avenue South
Minneapolis, MN 55419
www.jumplibrary.com

Copyright © 2025 Jump! International copyright reserved in all countries. No part of this book may be reproduced in any form without written permission from the publisher.

Library of Congress Cataloging-in-Publication Data

Names: Deniston, Natalie, author.
Title: Goose or duck? / by Natalie Deniston.
Description: Minneapolis, MN: Jump!, Inc., [2025]
Series: Spot the differences | Includes index.
Audience: Ages 5–8
Identifiers: LCCN 2024023297 (print)
LCCN 2024023298 (ebook)
ISBN 9798892136815 (hardcover)
ISBN 9798892136822 (paperback)
ISBN 9798892136839 (ebook)
Subjects: LCSH: Geese—Juvenile literature.
Ducks—Juvenile literature.
Classification: LCC QL696.A52 D455 2025 (print)
LCC QL696.A52 (ebook)
DDC 598.4/1—dc23/eng/20240620
LC record available at https://lccn.loc.gov/2024023297
LC ebook record available at https://lccn.loc.gov/2024023298

Editor: Katie Chanez
Designer: Emma Almgren-Bersie

Photo Credits: Mircea Costina/Shutterstock, cover (goose); steveo73/iStock, cover (duck); Phil Feyerabend/Shutterstock, 1 (left); Aksenova Natalya/Shutterstock, 1 (right), 21; Richard G Smith/Shutterstock, 3, 8–9, 23tr; JabaWeba/Shutterstock, 4; Rajesh_Nayak/Shutterstock, 5; Ljupco/iStock, 6–7 (top); Marc Bruxelle/Shutterstock, 6–7 (bottom); photosbyjimn/iStock, 10–11, 23tl, 23bl; Bernard Saumier/iStock, 12–13, 23br; blickwinkel/Alamy, 14–15; Frank Hecker/Alamy, 16–17; Gus Garcia/Shutterstock, 18–19; photomaster/Shutterstock, 20; pr2is/Shutterstock, 22 (left); Elena Krivorotova/Shutterstock, 22 (right); Adrian Eugen Ciobaniuc/Shutterstock, 24 (top); g images/Shutterstock, 24 (bottom).

Printed in the United States of America at Corporate Graphics in North Mankato, Minnesota.

Table of Contents

Water Birds 4
See and Compare 20
Quick Facts 22
Picture Glossary 23
Index 24
To Learn More 24

How to Use This Book

In this book, you will see pictures of both geese and ducks. Can you tell which one is in each picture?

Hint: You can find the answers if you flip the book upside down!

Water Birds

This is a goose.

This is a duck.

Both are birds.
They look alike.
But they are different.
How?
Let's see!

A goose's neck is long.
A duck's is short.
Which is this?

Answer: goose

Both have feathers.
A male goose's are dull.
A male duck's are bright.
Which is this?

Answer: duck

Both have webbed feet.
A goose's are often dark.
A duck's are often orange.
Whose feet are these?

Answer: goose

Both eat plants.

Ducks eat bugs and fish, too.

Which is this?

Answer: duck

Geese build nests in the open.

Ducks hide their nests in plants.

Whose nest is this?

Answer: duck

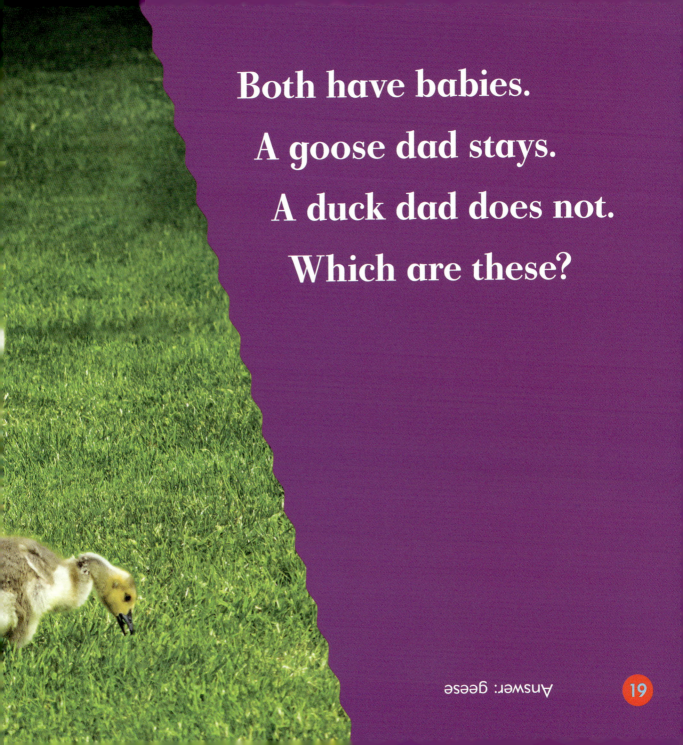

Both have babies.
A goose dad stays.
A duck dad does not.
Which are these?

Answer: geese

See and Compare

Goose

long neck

dull feathers

dark webbed feet

Duck

males have bright feathers

short neck

orange webbed feet

Quick Facts

Geese and ducks both live by water. They lay eggs. They are very similar. But they have some differences. Take a look!

Geese
- are bigger
- make honking sounds
- live mostly on land

Ducks
- are smaller
- make quacking sounds
- live mostly on water

Picture Glossary

bright
Bold and colorful and easy to see.

dull
Not bright.

feathers
The light, soft parts that cover a bird's body.

webbed
Connected by a fold of skin.

Index

babies 19
bugs 15
dad 19
eat 15
feathers 11
feet 12
fish 15
hide 16
male 11
neck 8
nests 16
plants 15, 16

To Learn More

Finding more information is as easy as 1, 2, 3.
❶ Go to www.factsurfer.com
❷ Enter "gooseorduck?" into the search box.
❸ Choose your book to see a list of websites.